Custodians
Yanuck, Debbie L. AR 2.5 LG

Custodians

by Debbie L. Yanuck

Consultant:
J. Kirk Campbell
Director of Maintenance and Custodial Services
Carleton College
Northfield, Minnesota

Bridgestone Books
an imprint of Capstone Press
Mankato, Minnesota

Bridgestone Books are published by Capstone Press
151 Good Counsel Drive, P.O. Box 669, Mankato, Minnesota 56002
www.capstonepress.com

Library of Congress Cataloging-in-Publication Data
Yanuck, Debbie L.
    Custodians/by Debbie L. Yanuck.
    p. cm.—(Community helpers)
    Includes bibliographical references and index.
    Summary: A simple introduction to the work custodians do, discussing where they
work, what tools they use, and how they are important to the communities they serve.
    ISBN-13: 978-0-7368-1127-9 (hardcover)
    ISBN-10: 0-7368-1127-3 (hardcover)
    1. Janitors—Juvenile literature. [1. Janitors. 2. Occupations.] I. Title. II. Community
helpers (Mankato, Minn.)
    TX339 .Y36 2002
    647'.2—dc21   2001003326

Editorial Credits
Megan Schoeneberger, editor; Karen Risch, product planning editor; Linda Clavel,
    cover production designer; Katy Kudela, photo researcher

Photo Credits
Capstone Press/Gregg Andersen, cover, 14, 20; Gary Sundermeyer, 4, 6, 12, 16
International Stock/Mark E. Gibson, 10
Shaffer Photography/James L. Shaffer, 8
Visuals Unlimited/Tom Uhlman, 18

1 2 3 4 5 6 07 06 05 04 03 02

Table of Contents

← FRONT LOUNGE

Custodians

Custodians keep buildings clean and in good shape. They clean schools and office buildings. They also clean shopping centers, hotels, and hospitals. They make sure office workers, teachers, and students have a clean place to work.

What Custodians Do

Custodians clean where people live, work, and learn. They pick up dirt from carpets with vacuum cleaners. They wash floors. Custodians dust furniture. They wipe sinks in bathrooms. They empty trash cans. Custodians change light bulbs and repair broken desks.

repair
to make something work again

Where Custodians Work

Custodians work in many places. Some custodians work indoors. They clean office buildings, schools, and hospitals. Other custodians work outdoors. They clean hotel pool areas and patios. They sometimes mow lawns.

patio
a paved area used for relaxing or eating outdoors

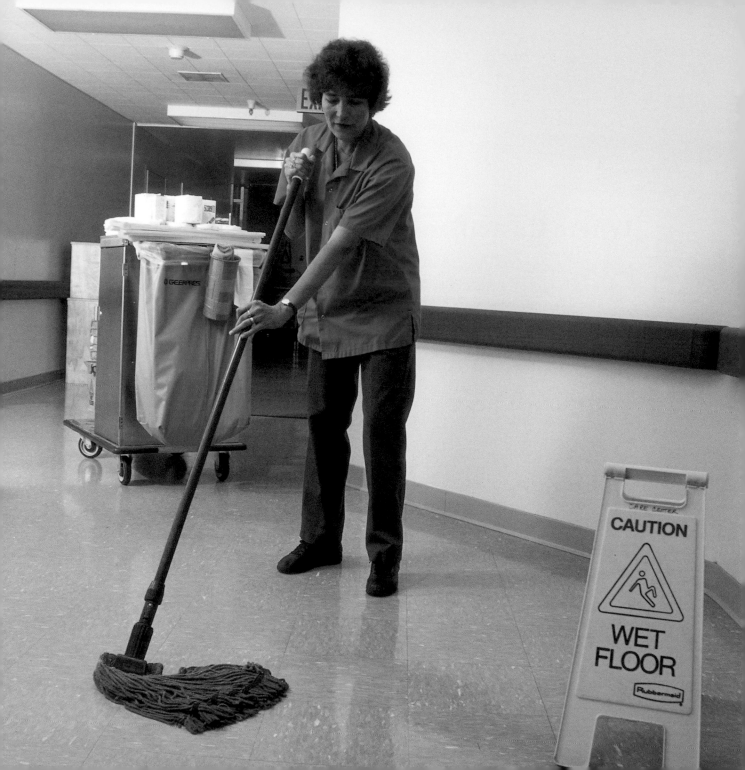

Tools Custodians Use

Custodians use many tools. They use mops and buckets. They sweep dirty floors with brooms. Custodians use wrenches to fix dripping faucets. They use screwdrivers to repair broken chairs. Custodians sometimes carry their supplies in rolling carts.

wrench
a tool with jaws used to tighten and loosen pipes

What Custodians Wear

Custodians wear clothing that keeps them safe. They wear shoes with rubber bottoms so they do not slip on wet floors. Custodians often wear rubber gloves. The gloves keep unsafe chemicals away from their hands. They sometimes wear masks on their faces.

chemical
a substance used in some cleaning products

School Custodians

School custodians clean schools. They make sure the bathrooms have enough paper towels and soap. They wipe the tables after students eat lunch. Some school custodians arrive early in the morning. Other school custodians work after the school day ends.

How Custodians Learn

Custodians learn by working on the job. They work with another custodian who has a lot of skill. Custodians learn to mix chemicals and to run polishing machines. They learn which types of cleaners to use for each job. Custodians must be able to understand directions.

People Who Help Custodians

Many people help custodians. Window washers clean windows on large buildings. Teachers and students try to keep classrooms neat. They throw away trash and push in their chairs at the end of the day.

How Custodians Help Others

Custodians clean buildings and keep them safe. They clean office buildings after workers go home. Custodians keep hospitals clean. They also keep schools clean and in good shape.

Hands On: Clean a Drawer

<u>What You Need</u>

A drawer
Trash can
Paper towels
Soapy water

<u>What You Do</u>

1. Pick a drawer to clean.
2. Empty the drawer.
3. Throw any trash from the drawer into the trash can.
4. Put some paper towels into the soapy water to make them wet.
5. Wipe out the inside of the drawer with the wet paper towels.
6. Dry the inside of the drawer with a dry paper towel.
7. Put everything neatly back into the drawer.
8. Throw the used paper towels into the trash can.

You can help custodians by keeping your desk clean at school and throwing trash into the trash can. You also can help custodians by thanking them for doing a good job.

Words to Know

chemical (KEM-uh-kuhl)—a substance used in some cleaning products

faucet (FAW-sit)—an object with a valve that is used to control the flow of water; people use faucets to turn water on and off.

machine (muh-SHEEN)—a tool made up of moving parts that is used to do a job

repair (ri-PAIR)—to make something work again; custodians repair broken chairs and faucets.

supplies (suh-PLYES)—items needed to do a job; custodians use cleaning supplies.

vacuum cleaner (VAK-yuhm KLEEN-ur)—a machine that picks up dirt; custodians use vacuum cleaners to pick up dirt from carpets and floors.

Read More

Kalman, Bobbie. *Community Helpers from A to Z.* AlphaBasiCs. New York: Crabtree Publishing, 1998.

Klingel, Cynthia Fitterer, and Robert B. Noyed. *School Custodians.* School Helpers. Vero Beach, Fla.: Rourke, 2001.

Internet Sites

NEA ESP-Custodial and Maintenance Services
http://www.nea.org/esp/jobs/custqual_1.htm
What Does a Custodian Do?
http://www.whatdotheydo.com/custodia.htm

Index